THE PURPOSE OF HISTORY

THE
PURPOSE OF HISTORY

BY

FREDERICK J. E. WOODBRIDGE

New York

COLUMBIA UNIVERSITY PRESS

1916

NOTE

This book contains three lectures delivered at the University of North Carolina on the McNair Foundation in March of the current year. It expresses certain conclusions about history to which I have been led by the study of the history of philosophy and by reflection on the work of contemporary philosophers, especially Bergson, Dewey, and Santayana.

I am happy to acknowledge my indebtedness to the Faculty and Students of the University of North Carolina for a most delightful visit at Chapel Hill.

F. J. E. W.

COLUMBIA UNIVERSITY
IN THE CITY OF NEW YORK
JUNE, 1916

CONTENTS

THE PURPOSE OF HISTORY

I

FROM HISTORY TO PHILOSOPHY

THE serious study of history is characteristic of a certain maturity of mind. For the intellectually young, the world is too new and attractive to arouse in them a very absorbing interest in its past. Life is for them an adventure, and the world is a place for excursions and experiences. They care little about what men have done, but much about what they might do. History, to interest them, must be written as a romance which will fire their imagination, rather than as a philosophy which might make them wise. But maturity, somewhat disciplined and disillusioned, confirms the suspicion, which even youth entertains at times, that the world, while offering an opportunity, hedges the offer about with restrictions which must be understood and submitted to, if effort is to be crowned with success. The mature may thus become eager to understand life without ceasing to enjoy it.

They may become philosophical and show their
wisdom by a desire to sympathize with what
men have done and to live rationally in the light
of what is possible. They may study history,
convinced that it enlarges their sympathies and
promotes rational living.

We might, therefore, conclude that the pre-
vailing interest in historical studies is a sign that
the age is growing in maturity and is seeking an
outlook upon life which is both sane and encour-
aging. This may well be true. But even if the
study of history indicate a certain maturity of
mind, it is not a guarantee that history will not
be studied in the spirit of youth. History may
do little more than afford a new world for wild
adventure and undisciplined experience. Moreover, maturity is not necessarily wise. Disgust,
revolt, and loss of sympathy are not always
strangers to it. Historical studies may be pur-
sued with little comprehension of their aim or
meaning; and history may be taught with little
reflection on its philosophical significance. It
would appear, therefore, that the study of
history itself affords an opportunity for philosophical inquiry, and may profitably stimulate
questions about the character of those facts with
which history is concerned.

2

FROM HISTORY TO PHILOSOPHY

In these lectures I intend to deal with the purpose of history. I would not, however, be misunderstood. My aim is not, by making another attempt to find the increasing purpose running through the ages, to win permanently the laurel which, hitherto, ambitious philosophers have worn only for a season. There is, no doubt, a kind of rapture in seeing history as St. Augustine saw it, — the progress of the City of God from earth to heaven; and there is a kind of pride not wholly ignoble, in seeing it as Hegel did, — the vibrating evolution from the brooding absolution of the East to the self-conscious freedom of one's own philosophy embraced and made universal by the civilizing energy of one's own state. My aim is more modest. It is not romantic, but technical. Metaphysics rather than poetry is to be my domain, although I cherish the hope that poetry may not, therefore, be misprized. If it may ultimately appear, not only as an ornament to living, but also as an exemplary method of living well, I may even now invoke the Muses to my aid, but Clio first, and, afterwards, Calliope. It is my aim, through an examination of what the historian himself proposes, to discover in what sense the idea of purpose in history is appropriate, and to what ideas

3

we are led when we think of history as the record
of human progress.

The conclusions I hope to clarify, I may here
anticipate. There is discoverable in history no
purpose, if we mean by purpose some future
event towards which the whole creation moves
and which past and present events portend; but
there is purpose in history, if we mean that
the past is utilized as material for the progressive
realization, at least by man, of what we call
spiritual ends. More generally, history is itself
essentially the utilization of the past for ends,
ends not necessarily foreseen, but ends to come,
so that every historical thing, when we view it
retrospectively, has the appearance of a result
which has been selected, and to which its antecedents are exclusively appropriate. In that
sense purpose is discoverable in history. But
this purpose is not single. History is pluralistic
and implies a pluralistic philosophy. There are
many histories, but no one of them exists to the
prejudice of any other. And, finally, progress is
not aptly conceived as an evolution from the past
into the future. Evolution is, rather, only a
name for historical continuity, and this continuity itself is a fact to be investigated and not
a theory which explains anything, or affords a

standard of value. The past is not the cause or beginning of the present, but the effect and result of history; so that every historical thing leaves, as it were, its past behind it as the record of its life in time. Progress may mean material progress when we have in mind the improvement in efficiency of the instruments man uses to promote his well-being; it may mean rational progress when we have in mind the idealization of his natural impulses. Then he frames in his imagination ideal ends which he can intelligently pursue and which, through the attempt to realize them, justify his labors. Such are the conclusions I hope to clarify, and I shall begin by considering the purpose men entertain when they write histories.

It is natural to quote Herodotus. The Father of History seems to have been conscious of his purpose and to have expressed it. We are told that he gave his history to the world "in order that the things men have done might not in time be forgotten, and that the great and wonderful deeds of both Greeks and barbarians might not become unheard of, — this, and why they fought with one another." This statement seems to be, in principle, an adequate expression of the purpose of writing histories, even if

Herodotus did not execute that purpose with fidelity. The limitations of its specific terms are obvious. One might expect that the great deeds were mainly exploits at arms, that the history would be military, and that the causes exposed would be causes of war. But the history itself deals with geography and climate, with manners, customs, traditions, and institutions, fully as much as with heroes and battles. Professor Gilbert Murray says of it: "His work is not only an account of a thrilling struggle, politically very important, and spiritually tremendous; it is also, more perhaps than any other known book, the expression of a whole man, the representation of all the world seen through the medium of one mind and in a particular perspective. The world was at that time very interesting; and the one mind, while strongly individual, was one of the most comprehensive known to human records. Herodotus's whole method is highly subjective. He is too sympathetic to be consistently critical, or to remain cold towards the earnest superstitions of people about him: he shares from the outset their tendency to read the activity of a moral God in all the moving events of history. He is sanguine, sensitive, a lover of human nature, interested in details if they are vital to his story, oblivious of them if they are only facts and figures; he catches quickly the atmosphere of the society he moves in, and falls readily under the spell of great human influences, the solid impersonal Egyptian hierarchy or the dazzling circle of great individuals at Athens; yet all the time shrewd, cool, gentle in judgment, deeply and unconsciously convinced of the weakness of human nature, the flaws of its heroism and the excusableness of its apparent villainy. His book bears for good and ill the stamp of this character and this profession." [1]

The history of Herodotus would, then, preserve a record of the world of human affairs as he discovered it and an exposition of the causes and conditions which have influenced human action. He would record what men have done in order that their deeds might be remembered and in order that they might be understood. Like all other historians he had his individual limitations, but for all of them he seems to have expressed the purpose of their inquiries. That purpose may be worked out in many different fields. We may have military history, political history,

---

[1] Murray, Gilbert. "Ancient Greek Literature." D. Appleton & Co., 1908. Page 133.

industrial history, economic history, religious history, the history of civilization, of education, and of philosophy, the history, indeed, of any human enterprise whatever. But always the purpose is the same, to preserve a faithful record and to promote the understanding of what has happened in the affairs of men. I need hardly add that, for the present, I am restricting history to human history. Its wider signification will not be neglected, but I make the present limitation in order that through a consideration of the writing of human history, we may be led on to the conception of history in its more comprehensive form.

To conceive the purpose of writing history adequately is not the same thing as to execute that purpose faithfully. If Herodotus may be cited in illustration of the adequate conception, he will hardly be cited by historians in illustration of its faithful execution. They have complained of him from time to time ever since Thucydides first accused him of caring more about pleasing his readers than about telling the truth. He is blamed principally for his credulity and for his lack of criticism. Credulous he was and less critical than one could wish, but it is well to remember, in any just estimate of him, that he was much less credulous and much more critical than we should naturally expect a man of his time to be. He wrote in an age when men generally believed spontaneously things which we, since we reflect, can not believe, and when it was more congenial to listen to a story than to indulge in the criticism of it. He frequently expresses disbelief of what he has been told and is often at great pains to verify what he has heard. With all his faults he remains among the extraordinary men.

These faults, when they are sympathetically examined, indicate far less blemishes in the character of Herodotus than they do the practical and moral difficulties which beset the faithful writing of all history. That is why he is so illustrative for our purpose. A faithful and true record is the first thing the historian desires, but it is a very difficult thing to obtain. Human testimony even in the presence of searching cross-examination is notoriously fallible, and the dumb records of the past, with all their variations and contradictions, present a stolid indifference to our curiosity. The questions we ask of the dead, only we ourselves can answer. Herodotus wrote with these practical and moral difficulties at a maximum. We have learned systematically to combat them. There has grown up for our benefit an abundant literature which would instruct the historian how best to proceed. The methods of historians, their failures and successes, have been carefully studied with the result that we have an elaborate science of writing history which we call historiography. Therein one may learn how to estimate sources, deal with documents, weigh evidence, detect causes, and be warned against the errors to which one is liable. Moreover, anthropology, archæology, and psychology have come to the historian's aid to help him in keeping his path as clear and unobstructed as possible. In other words, history has become more easy and more difficult to write than it was in the days of Herodotus. The better understanding of its difficulties and of the ways to meet them has made it more easy; but the widening of its scope has made it more difficult. We still face the contrast between the adequate conception of the purpose of writing history and the faithful execution of that purpose. But it would seem that only practical and moral difficulties stand in the way of successful performance. Ideally, at least, a perfect history seems to be conceivable.

It is, indeed, conceivable that with adequate

data, with a wise and unbiased mind, and with a moderate supply of genius, an historian might faithfully record the events with which he deals, and make us understand how they happened. It is conceivable because it has in many cases been so closely approximated. Our standards of judgment and appraisement here are doubtless open to question by a skeptical mind. We may lack the evidence which would make our estimate conclusive. But what I mean is this: histories have been written which satisfy to a remarkable degree the spirit of inquiry. They present that finality and inevitability which mark the master mind. There are, in other words, authorities which few of us ever question. They have so succeeded, within their limitations, in producing the sense of adequacy, that their reputation seems to be secure. Their limitations have been physical, rather than moral or intellectual, so that the defects which mar their work are less their own than those of circumstance. They thus appear to be substantial witnesses that the only difficulties in the way of faithfully executing the purpose of writing history are practical and moral — to get the adequate data, the wise and unbiased mind, and the moderate supply of genius. There are no other difficulties.

Yet when we say that there are no other difficulties we may profitably bear in mind that Herodotus has been charged not only with being credulous and uncritical, but also with not telling the truth. At first this might not appear to indicate a new difficulty. For if Herodotus lied, his difficulty was moral. But it is not meant that Herodotus lied. It is meant rather that within his own limitations he did not, and possibly could not, give us the true picture of the times which he recorded. He saw things too near at hand to paint them in that perspective which truthfully reveals their proportions. His emphases, his lights and shadows, are such as an enlightened man of his time might display, but they are not the emphases, the lights and shadows which, as subsequent historians have proved, give us ancient Greece with its true shading. We understand his own age much better than he did because Grote and other moderns have revealed to us what Greece really was. But what, we may ask, was the real Greece? Who has written and who can write its true history? Grote's reputation as an historian is secure, but his history has already been superseded in many important respects. We are told that, since its publication, "a great

12

change has come over our knowledge of Greek civilization." What then shall we say if neither Herodotus, who saw that civilization largely face to face, nor Grote, who portrays it after an exceptionally patient and thorough study of its records, supplemented by what he calls scientific criticism and a positive philosophy, has given us the real Greece? Clearly it looks as if the perfect history is yet to be written, and as if every attempt to write it pushes it forward into the future. And clearly we face, if not a new difficulty, a fact at least which is of fundamental importance in the attempt to understand what history itself is.

So Herodotus becomes again illustrative. His history once written and given to the world becomes itself an item in the history of Greece, making it necessary that the story be retold. In the face of a fact, at once so simple and so profound, how idle is the boast of the publisher who could say of the author of a recent life of Christ [1] that she "has reproduced the time of Christ, not as we would understand it, but as He himself saw it. She has told what He believed and did, rather than what He is reported to have said. She has stripped Him of tradition

[1] Austin, Mary. "The Man Jesus." Harper, 1915.

and shown Him as He was; she has given to literature an imperishable figure, not of the wan Galilean of the Middle Ages, but of the towering figure of all history." How idle, I repeat, is such a boast of finality when we know that this new history of Christ, instead of ending the matter, may cause another history to be written by some student who comes to the old record with a new insight and a new inspiration. It is possible, we may say, to portray the Christ of His own day, or the wan Galilean of the Middle Ages, or the figure which commands the attention of the twentieth century, but the real Christ, the towering figure of all history, — who will portray that? It is yet to be done and done again. No historical fact can ever have its history fully written: and this, not because the adequate data, the wise and unbiased mind, and the moderate supply of genius are lacking, but because it is itself the producer of new history the more it is historically understood. It grows, it changes, it expands the more adequately we apparently grasp it. We seem never to be at the end of its career and we must stop abruptly with its history still unfinished. Others may take up our task, but they will end as we have ended. The history of nothing is complete.

14

It is well-nigh impossible to avoid the suspicion of paradox in such statements as these. Yet I feel confident that every historical student keenly alive to his task is abundantly sensible of this truth. Where will he end the history of Greece or of Rome? What will be the final chapter of the French Revolution? No: there is no paradox here, but there is an ambiguity. For history is not only a record written to preserve memory and promote understanding, it is also a process in time. "With us," Professor Flint writes, "the word 'history,' like its equivalents in all modern languages, signifies either a form of literary composition or the appropriate subject or matter of such composition — either a narrative of events, or events which may be narrated. It is impossible to free the term of this doubleness and ambiguity of meaning. Nor is it, on the whole, to be desired. The advantages of having one term which may, with ordinary caution, be innocuously applied to two things so related, more than counterbalance the dangers involved in two things so distinct having the same name. The history of England which actually happened can not easily be confounded with the history of England written by Mr. Green; while by the latter being termed history as well as the former, we are reminded that it is an attempt to reproduce or represent the course of the former. Occasionally, however, the ambiguity of the word gives rise to great confusion of thought and gross inaccuracy of speech. And this occurs most frequently, if not exclusively, just when men are trying and professing to think and speak with especial clearness and exactness regarding the signification of history — i.e., when they are labouring to define it. Since the word history has two very different meanings, it obviously can not have merely one definition. To define an order of facts and a form of literature in the same terms — to suppose that when either of them is defined the other is defined — is so absurd that one would probably not believe it could be seriously done were it not so often done. But to do so has been the rule rather than the exception. The majority of so-called definitions of history are definitions only of the records of history. They relate to history as narrated and written, not to history as evolved and acted; in other words, although given as the only definitions of history needed, they do not apply to history itself, but merely to accounts of history. They may tell us what constitutes a book of history, but they can not tell us what the history is with which all books of history are occupied. It is, however, with history in this latter sense that a student of the science or philosophy of history is mainly concerned." [1]

It is because history is not only something "narrated and written," but also something "evolved and acted" that we are led to say that the history of nothing is complete. The narrative may begin and end where we please; and might conceivably, within its scope, be adequate. But the beginning and the end of the action are so interwoven with the whole time process that adequacy here becomes progressive. That is the fundamental reason why Grote's history surpasses that of Herodotus in what we call historical truth. For the truth of history is a progressive truth to which the ages as they continue contribute. The truth for one time is not the truth for another, so that historical truth is something which lives and grows rather than something fixed to be ascertained once for all. To remember what has happened, and to understand it, carries us thus to the recognition that the writing of history is itself an historical process. It, too, is something "evolved and

[1] Flint, Robert. "History of the Philosophy of History." Charles Scribner's Sons, 1894. Page 5.

acted." It is perennially fresh even if the events with which it deals are long since past and gone. The record may be final, but our understanding of what has been recorded can make no such claim. The accuracy of the record is not the truth of history. We are well assured, for instance, that the Greeks defeated the Persians at the battle of Marathon in 490 B.C. The record on that point is not seriously questionable, although we have to rely on documents which have had a precarious fortune. And, coming to our own day, we can have little doubt that the record of this greater Marathon of Europe will surpass all others in fulness and accuracy. There are, indeed, as Thucydides pointed out long ago, difficulties in the way of exactness even when we are dealing with contemporaneous events. "Eye-witnesses of the same events speak differently as their memories or their sympathies vary." Such difficulties we have learned how to check until our records closely approach truth of fact. Consequently the records of what men have done, or may be doing, may be relatively unimpeachable. But it is quite a different matter to understand what they have done and are doing. Without that understanding, history is no better than a chronicle, a table of events, but not that

18

"thing to possess and keep always" after which the historian aspires.

To understand is not simply difficult, it is also endless. But this fact does not make it hopeless. The understanding of history grows by what it feeds on, enlarges itself with every fresh success, constantly reveals more to be understood. Our illustrations may serve us again. From the accessible records of the battle of Marathon we can understand with tolerable success the immediate antecedents and consequents of that great event. But in calling the event great we do not simply eulogize its participants. We indicate, rather, that its antecedents and consequents have been far-reaching and momentous. Greece, we say, was saved. But what are we to understand by that salvation? To answer we must write and rewrite her own history, the history of what she has been and is; and with every fresh writing the battle of Marathon becomes better understood. It becomes a different battle with a different truth. And more than this: with every rewriting we understand better what went before and what followed after until the battle itself becomes but the symptom of deeper things. So, too, is it with Europe's present struggle. Already its history has begun

19

with many volumes. Following the example of Thucydides in the Peloponnesian war, men are writing it contemporaneously by summers and winters. The consequences they can only guess at, but they have done much with the antecedents, so much that the last fifty years of Europe are better understood than they were a year ago. The record of them has changed little; our understanding of them has changed much. It has changed so much that they have already become a different half-century from what they were. The truth about them last year is not the the truth about them to-day. Fifty years hence what will the truth about them be?

I venture another illustration, one from the history of philosophy. I choose Plato. He is such a commanding figure that the desire to understand him is exceptionally keen. The record of his life and of his conscious aims and purposes is very unsatisfactory. We have no assured authorities on these points. That is greatly to be regretted, because a correct record is naturally the best of aids towards a correct understanding. But the unsatisfactory record is not very material to the illustration in hand. The record might be correct, but Plato would, even so, remain an historical figure to be understood. He would continue to be the producer of what we call Platonism, and we should have to understand him as that producer. In that case, evidently, the details of his life, his span of years, his immediate aims and activities would involve but the beginning of an inquiry which would last as long as Plato is studied by those who would understand him. Who, then, would be the real Plato? The man about whom Aristotle wrote, or the man about whom Professor Paul Shorey writes? Undoubtedly the real Plato is the man about whom they both write, but that can mean only that he is the man about whom writers can write so diversely. He is not the same man to Professor Shorey that he was to Aristotle; and it is, consequently, a nice question which of the two disciples has given us the correct estimate of their master. Who was the real Plato? And that question could still be asked even if the Platonic tradition were in its record, what it is not, a continuous and uniformly accepted tradition. For it is quite evident that the Platonic tradition has grown from age to age as students of Plato have tried to understand him and to understand also what other students have understood about him. The true Plato is still the quest of Platonists.

It seems clear, therefore, that historical truth, if we do not mean by that simply the truth of the records with which we deal, is something which can not be ascertained once for all. It is a living and dynamic truth. It is genuinely progressive. We may say that it is like something being worked out in the course of time, and something which the sequence of events progressively exposes or makes clear. If, therefore, we declare that Herodotus, or any other historian, has not told the truth, and do not mean thereby that he has uttered falsehoods, we mean only that the truth has grown beyond him and his time. For his time it might well be that he told the truth sufficiently. Ancient Greece may then have been precisely what he said it was. To blame him for not telling us what ancient Greece is now, is to blame him irrationally. In the light of historical truth, the Father of History and all his children have been, not simply historians of times old and new, but also contributors to that truth and progressive revealers of it. If they have been faithful to their professed purpose of preserving the memory of what has happened and in making what has happened understood, they are not rivals in the possession of truth. They have all been associated in a common enterprise, that of conserving the history of man in order that what that history is and what it implies may be progressively better known.

History is therefore not simply the telling of what has happened; it is also and more profoundly the conserving of what has happened in order that its meaning may be grasped. A book of history differs radically from a museum of antiquities. In the museum, the past is preserved, but it is a dead past, the flotsam and jetsam of the stream of time. It may afford material for history, and then it is quickened into life. In a book of history, the past lives. It is in a very genuine sense progressive. It grows and expands with every fresh study of it, because every fresh study of it puts it into a larger, a more comprehensive, and a new perspective, and makes its meaning ever clearer. The outcome of reflections like these is that history is constantly revealing something like an order or purpose in human affairs, a truth to which they are subject and which they express. History is, therefore, a career in time. That is why no historical item can be so placed and dated that the full truth of it is definitely prescribed and limited to that place and date. Conformably with the calendar and with geography we may be able to affirm that a given event was or is taking place, but to tell what that event is in a manner which ensures understanding of it, is to write the history of its career in time as comprehensively as it can be written. It is to conserve that event, not as an isolated and detached specimen of historical fact, but as something alive which, as it continues to live, reveals more and more its connections in the ceaseless flow of history itself.

The writer of history may, consequently, attain his purpose within the limits of the practical and moral difficulties which beset it in either of two ways. He may give us the contemporaneous understanding of what has happened in terms of the outlook and perspective of his own day, giving us a vision of what has gone before as an enlightened mind of his time might see it. His history might then be that of ancient peoples beheld in the new perspective into which they have now been placed. Could he, by miracle, recall the ancients back to life, they would doubtless fail to recognize their own history, truthful as it might be. But comprehension might dawn upon them as they read, and they might exclaim: "These were the things we were really doing, but we did not know it at the time;

we have discovered what we were; our history has revealed to us ourselves." Or the historian, by the restrained exercise of his imagination, may give us what has happened in the perspective of the time in which it happened, or in a perspective anterior to his own day. He may seek to recover the sense, so to speak, of past contemporaneity, transplanting us in imagination to days no longer ours and to ways of feeling and acting no longer presently familiar. Such a history would be less comprehensive and complete than the former. It would also be more difficult to write, because historical imagination of this kind is rare and also because it is not easy to divest the past of its present estimate. Yet the imagination has that power and enables us to live again in retrospect what others have lived before us. But in both cases the history would be an active conservation of events in time; it would reveal their truth, their meaning, and their purpose.

If now we ask what may be this truth and meaning, or in what sense may we appropriately speak of a purpose in history, we pass from history to philosophy. No longer shall we be concerned with the purpose of writing history, but rather with the character of the facts which stimulate that purpose and assist in its attainment. From history as the attempt to preserve memory and promote understanding we pass to history as a characteristic of natural processes. We shall try to analyze what the career of things in time involves; but we shall keep this career in mind in those aspects of it which bear most significantly upon the history of man.

II

THE PLURALISM OF HISTORY

HISTORY leads to philosophy when it raises in a fundamental way the question of truth. As we have seen, the term "truth," when applied to history, has a double meaning. It may mean that the record of what has happened is correct, and it may mean that the understanding of what has happened is correct. If the record is correct, its truth seems to be something fixed once for all and unchanging. The perfect record may never be possessed, but it seems to be ideally possible, because the events which the record would keep in memory must have happened, and, therefore, might have been recorded if fortune had been favorable. If, however, the understanding of what has happened is correct, its truth can not be something fixed once for all. It is fixed only from time to time. One correct understanding of what has happened does not displace another as truth might displace error, but one supplements and enlarges another. Histories which have gone before are not undone by those that follow after. They are incorporated into them in a very real way. Historical truth, therefore, when it does not mean simply the correctness of the records of history, is progressive. If the record of what has happened is correct, its truth is perpetual; if the understanding of what has happened is correct, its truth is contemporaneous. Now what does this distinction involve? Does it involve merely the recognition that facts may remain unchanged while our knowledge of them grows? A suspicion, at least, has been created that it involves something more, namely, the recognition that the facts themselves, being something "evolved and acted," are also progressive. Historical facts are careers in time. It is their occurrence which is recorded and it is their career which is understood. We may, therefore, undertake an inquiry into the nature of facts like these.

We may start from the distinction between facts and our knowledge of them, for it is clear that whatever the character of the facts may be, our knowledge of them, at least, is progressive. The past is dead and gone. It is something over and done with, so that any change in it is forever impossible. We should then, if we would be precise, say, not that it is the past

28

which grows and enlarges, but only our knowledge of it. We recover and conserve it in memory and imagination only, and as we recover it more and more completely and relate it more and more successfully, we know and understand it better. Plato is dead, and not one feature, circumstance, or action of his life can now be changed. He lives only in the memory of man; and because he lives there and stimulates the imagination, there is born a Plato of the imagination. There are thus two Platos, the one real and the other historical. The one lived and died long ago; the other still lives in human history. The real Plato has produced the historical Plato and affords a check upon historians in their representation of him. That representation may approach progressively nearer to what the real Plato was like, but it can never be the man who has passed away. History would be thus a branch of human knowledge, and grow with the growth of knowledge, while its objects remain unchanged. That is why history has constantly to be rewritten. Furthermore, in the rewriting, new types of history appear with new or altered emphases. The moral and religious type is supplemented by the political, and the political by the economic and social. For with the growth of knowledge the past looks different to us and we discover that what appeared once adequate has to be revised.

We may admit, therefore, that history, whatever else it may be, is at any rate a kind of human knowledge. Like all knowledge it leads us to recognize that there is a distinction between knowledge itself and its objects, and that the progressive character of knowledge indicates an approximation to an adequate representation of the objects and not changes in their own character. This distinction in its application to history is evidently not a distinction between literature and its subject-matter. For the past, if we now take the past to be the proper subject-matter of written history, appears to have a twofold character. It is all that has happened precisely as it happened, and it is all that is remembered and known, precisely as it is remembered and known. There are, we may say, a real past and an historical past. The latter never is the former, but always a progressively more adequate representation of the former.

Now this distinction between the real past and the historical past may be fruitful. It may also be treacherous, for the terms in which it is expressed are treacherous terms. For it is very

30

easy to claim that the real past is after all only the historical past, because the past itself being dead and gone is now real only as it is preserved in history. Yet properly understood, the distinction is essential to any philosophical comprehension of what history is. It points out that history is not the past, but is its recovery and conservation. Events begin and end; men are born and die; events and men disappear into the past in a manner and an order which are unalterable. But it is not their disappearance which constitutes their existence in time a history. Their historical existence is a kind of continuing life. It may be that it continues only in human knowledge, but, even so, it clearly illustrates the nature of history as a process in time. In other words the life of knowledge, of memory and imagination, is itself a continual recording of what has happened, a continual understanding of it, and a continual putting of it in a new and enlarged perspective. Here, too, within the narrow limits of man's perceiving and comprehending life to which we have now restricted history, events begin and end, men are born and die, and events and men disappear into the past in a manner and an order which are unalterable. Yet even as they disappear never

31

to return in the precise and identical manner of their first existence, they are conserved, and continue the process of dying as occurrences in order to live as a history. Yesterday as yesterday is gone forever. Its opportunities are over and its incidents dead. As an historical yesterday it lives as material for to-day's employment. It becomes an experience to profit by, a mistake to remedy, or a success to enjoy. History is thus the great destroyer and the great preserver. We must speak of it in apparent paradoxes. The child becomes a man only by ceasing to be a child; Plato becomes an historical figure only by dying; whatever happens is conserved only by being first destroyed.

But the conservation of what happens is obviously not a perpetuation. History is not the staying of events, for time forbids that they stay. The conservation is rather a utilization, a kind of employment or working over of material. Through it discriminations and selections are made and connections discovered; the moving panorama is converted into an order of events which can be understood, because consequences are seen in the light of their antecedents and antecedents are seen in the light of the consequences to which they lead. There is thus a genuine incorporation of what has happened into what does happen, of yesterday into to-day, so that yesterday becomes a vital part of to-day and finds its enlargement and fulfilment there. We can thus write our own biographies. It is possible for us to discover what mistakes we have made and what ends we have attained. Our history appears thus to be a utilization of material, a realization of ends, a movement with purpose in it. Selection is characteristic of it very profoundly. Other histories, of other men, of times, of peoples, of institutions, we write in the same way because in the same way we discover and understand what has happened in their case. Such a destroying, conserving, utilizing, selective, and purposeful movement in time, history appears to be when we restrict it to the domain of human knowledge.

It seems, however, idle so to restrict it. For other things besides our knowledge grow — animals and plants, and the stars even. They, too, have a history, and it may be that their history, being also an affair in time, is not unlike in character to our own growth in knowledge. Or perhaps it were even better to say that both they and our knowledge illustrate equally what history is, discovering time itself to be the great historian. All time-processes, that is, appear to be, when we attentively consider them, processes which supplement, complete, or transform what has gone before. They are active conservations and utilizations of the past as material. They save what has happened from being utterly destroyed, and, in saving it, complete and develop it. Time is, thus, constantly rounding out things, so to speak, or bringing them to some end or fulfilment. That is why we call its movement purposeful.

Time

Yet there have been philosophies which have tried to make of time a magical device by which man might represent to himself in succession that which in itself is never in succession. They picture his journey through life as a journey through space where all that he sees, one thing after another, comes successively into view like the houses on a street along which he may walk. But as the houses do not exist in succession, neither do the facts he discovers. They, too, come into view as he moves along. These philosophies, consequently, would have us think of a world in itself, absolute and complete, to which nothing can be added and from which nothing can be subtracted. It is somehow fixed and finished now; but our human experience, being incomplete and unfinished, gives to it the appearance of a process in time and discloses to us what it would be like if all its factors and the laws which hold them in perfect equilibrium were experienced in succession. History would thus be a kind of temporal revelation of the absolute and we should read it as we read a book, from cover to cover, discovering page by page a story which is itself finished when we begin.

Or philosophy, when it has not conceived the world to be thus finished and complete in itself and only appearing to us as a temporal revelation, has often thought of movements in time as only the results of preceding movements. Whatever happens is thus conceived to be the effect of what has already happened, rather than the active conservation and working over of what has already happened. The past is made the cause and producer of the present, so that the state of the world at any moment is only the result or outcome of what it was in the preceding moment. To-day is thought to be the effect of yesterday and the cause of to-morrow, and is thus but a transition from one day to another. Time-processes are thus robbed of any genuine activity or productivity, and time itself is made to be nothing but the sequential order in which events occur. Purpose, conservation, utilization, and all that active supplementing and working over of the past on which we have dwelt, become illusions when applied to the world at large. They represent our way of conceiving things, but not nature's way of doing things.

But these philosophies, as Professor Bergson especially among recent philosophers has pointed out,[1] gain whatever force they have principally from the fact that they think of time in terms of space. They picture it as a line already drawn, when they should picture it as a line in the process of being drawn. As already drawn, the line has a beginning, an end, and consequently, a middle point. Let us call the middle point the present. All the line to the left of that point we will call the past and all to the right of it the future. We thus behold time spatially with all its parts coexistent as the points on the line. Events are then conceived to move from the past through the present into the future, just

[1] See especially his "Données immédiates de la conscience," 1888. (Eng. tr. "Time and Free Will," by F. L. Pogson. The Macmillan Company, 1912.) "L'évolution créatrice," 1908. (Eng. tr. "Creative Evolution," by Arthur Mitchell. Henry Holt and Company, 1913.)

as a pencil point may pass from the beginning of the line through its middle point to the end. But, unlike the pencil point, they can not go backward. This fact gives us a characteristic by which we may distinguish time from space even if we have represented time spatially. The spatial order is reversible, the temporal is not. Time is like a line on which you can go forward, but on which you can not go backward. But you can go forward. Everything goes from the past to the future. The present is but the transition point of their going.

There are, undoubtedly, advantages in thinking of time in this spatial way. Thereby we are able to make calendars and have a science of mechanics. It affords a basis for many successful predictions. But, quite evidently, time is neither such a line nor anything like it. Nothing whatever goes from the past through the present into the future. We can not make such a statement intelligible. For "to go" from the past to the future is not like going from New York to Boston. Boston is already there to go to, but the future is not anywhere to go to. And New York is there to leave, but the past is not anywhere to leave. What then is this mysterious "going" if its starting-point and its end are both non-existent now? Clearly it is a "going" only in a metaphorical sense. We call it a "going" because we can so represent it by dates and places. We can say that here we have been going from Friday through Saturday to Sunday. But it is quite clear that to-day is neither past nor future, that it is neither yesterday nor to-morrow, and that if we go anywhere we must start to-day. When Sunday comes, Saturday will be yesterday. But note now the strange situation into which we have fallen — only in the future is this day ever in the past! And that is true of every day in the world's history. It becomes a past day only in its own future.

Clearly then time is not like a line already drawn. It is more like a line in the drawing. You take the pencil and the line is left behind it as the pencil moves. New points are being constantly added to what has gone before. The line is being manufactured. Let us call so much of it as has now been drawn the past and that which has not yet been drawn the future. It is clear then that the present is not the middle point of the line nor any point whatever upon it, for all of the line that has been drawn belongs to the past and all the rest of it to the future. Its past has already been done; its future is not yet done, but only possible. Futhermore, it is clear that no point moves from the past into the future. Such a movement is unintelligible. If there is any movement of points at all, it is a movement into the past. That is, the line, instead of growing into the future, grows into the past — continually more and more of it is drawn. For remember that the future of the line is not the place on the paper or in the air which by and by the line may occupy. Its future is a genuine future, a possibility as yet nowhere realized. It is the part of the line which always will be, but never is; or, better, it is that part of the line which will have a place and a date if the line continues to be drawn. The movement of time is thus not a movement from the past to the future, but from the possible to the actual, from what may be to what has been. The present is not the vanishing point between past and future; it is not, so to speak, in the same line or dimension with them. It is something quite different. It is all that we mean by activity or eventuality. It is the concrete, definite, and effective transforming of the possible into the actual. It is the *drawing* of the line, but in no sense is it a part or point of the line itself.

There are, doubtless, difficulties in thinking

of time in this way, for it is not entirely free from spatial reminiscences. But it serves to point out that past, present, and future are not like parts of a whole into which an absolute or complete time is divided. They are more like derivatives of the time process itself in the concrete instances of its activity. They are what every growing or changing thing involves, whether it be the knowledge of man or the crust of the earth, for everything that grows or changes manufactures a past by realizing a future. It leaves behind it the record of what it has done conserved by memory or by nature, and in leaving that record behind constantly enlarges or transforms it. The growth moves in a manner and an order which when once performed are unalterable, but there is growth none the less. Since time is like this, it seems evidently unintelligible to restrict it and history to human experience and make the world in itself absolute. It would be better to say that it is history in the large sense applicable to the world itself that makes human experience possible. Yet it would be more advisable not to make such a distinction at all, but to recognize that human experience is one kind of history, namely, history conscious of itself, the time process deliberately at work.

40

Now it is evident that history in this latter sense is purposive and selective. That which has happened is not remembered as a whole or understood as a whole. Not only are details forgotten or neglected, but things and events otherwise important are omitted for the sake of securing emphasis and distinction among the things remembered. Herodotus spoke of "wonderful deeds" and others following this example have regarded history as concerned only with great men and great events. It is true that the little men and the little events tend to disappear, but we should remember that it is the selective character of history which makes them little. Speaking absolutely, we may say that no item, however apparently insignificant, is really insignificant in the historical development of any people or any institution, for in some measure every item is material to that development. But all are not equally material. The absence of any one of them might undoubtedly have changed the whole history, but given the presence of them all, some are of greater significance than others.

The history of the English people may be regarded as a development of personal liberty. It is doubtless more than that, but it is that.

41

As such a development, it is evident that there are many things which an historian of personal liberty will disregard in order that the particular movement he is studying may be emphasized and distinguished. It will be that particular movement which will determine for him what is great and what little. So it comes about that histories are diversified even when they are histories of the same thing. There are many histories of England which differ from one another not only in accuracy, philosophical grasp, and brilliancy, but also in the purpose they discover England to be fulfilling. By purpose here is not meant a predestined end which England is bound to reach, but the fact that her history can be construed as a development of a specific kind. In other words her past can be understood only when it is seen to be relevant to some particular career which has its termination in her existing institutions. Her past has contributed through time to definite results which are now apparent. The things that have happened have not all contributed to these results in the same measure. Some have contributed more, some less. What is true in this illustration appears to be true generally. Every history is a particular career in the development of which some facts, persons, and events have been more significant than others, so that the termination of the career at any time is like an end that has been reached or a consequence to which its antecedents are peculiarly appropriate. That is the sense in which history is purposeful and selective.

The selection is twofold. First, there is selection of the type of career, and secondly, there is selection of the items especially relevant to its progress. We may have the military, the political, the social, the industrial, the economic, or the religious history of England, for instance, and although these histories will overlap and involve one another, each of them will exhibit a career which is peculiar and distinct from its fellows. When reading the industrial history we shall not be reading the religious history. In the one we shall find circumstances and events recorded which we do not find in the other, because all circumstances and events do not have significance equally for the development of industry and religion. Historical selection is, therefore, twofold, — the selection of a career to be depicted and of events and circumstances peculiarly relevant to that career.

Is this selection, we may ask, only a device

on the historian's part to facilitate our comprehension, or is it a genuine characteristic of the time process itself? Does the historian read purpose into history or does he find it there? It may assist in answering such questions to observe that if selection is a device of the historian, it is one to which he is compelled. Without it history is unintelligible. Unless we understand events and circumstances as contributing to a definite result and contributing in different measures, we do not understand them at all. The Magna Charta, the British Constitution, the Tower of London, the River Thames, the mines of Wales, the plays of Shakespeare — all these things and things like them are for us quite unintelligible if they illuminate no career or illustrate no specific movements to which they have particularly contributed. Selection is, consequently, not a device which the historian has invented; it is imposed upon him by his own purpose to preserve the memory and promote the understanding of what has happened. The procedure of the historian is not arbitrary, but necessary. It is imposed upon him by the character of the facts with which he deals. These facts are movements from the possible to the actual and are helped and hindered by other such movements. An historical fact is not only spread out in space and exists equally with all its contemporaries at an assignable place in reference to them, it also persists in time, comes before and after other persisting facts, and persists along with others in a continuance equal to, or more or less than, theirs. In a figure we may say, facts march on in time, but not all at the same speed or with the same endurance; they help or impede one another's movement; they do not all reach the goal; some of them turn out to be leaders, others followers; their careers overlap and interfere; so that the result is a failure for some and a success for others. The march is their history.

This is figure, but it looks like the fact. Simple illustrations may enforce it. The seeds which we buy and sow in the spring are not simply so many ounces of chemical substances. They are also so many possible histories or careers in time, so many days of growth, so much promise of fruit or flower. Each seed has its own peculiar history with its own peculiar career. The seeds are planted. Then in the course of time, soil and moisture and atmosphere and food operate in unequal ways in the development of each career. Each is furthered or hindered as events fall out. Some careers are cut short, others prosper. Everywhere there is selection. Everywhere there is adaptation of means to ends. The history of the garden can be written because there is a history there to write.

Such an illustration can be generalized. Our world is indubitably a world in time. That means much more than the fact that its events can be placed in accordance with a map or dated in accordance with a calendar. It means that they are events in genuine careers, each with its own particular character and its own possibility of a future, like the seeds in the garden. Things with histories have not only structures in space and are, accordingly, related geometrically to one another; they have not only chemical structures and are thus analyzable into component parts; they have also structures in time. They are not now what they will be, but what they will be is always continuous with what they are, so that we must think of them stretched out, so to speak, in time as well as in space, or as being so many moments as well as so much volume. What they become, however, depends not only on their own time structures, but also on their interplay with one another. They are helped and hindered in their development. The results reached at any time are such as complete those which have gone before, for each career is the producer, but not the product of its past.

It seems clear, therefore, that there is purpose in history. But "purpose" is a troublesome word. It connotes design, intention, foresight, as well as the converging of means upon a specific end. Only in the latter sense is it here used, but with this addition: the end is to be conceived not in terms of any goal ultimately reached, but in terms of the career of which it is the termination; and in this career, the present is continually adding to and completing the past. The growing seeds end each in its own specific flower or fruit. They are each of its own kind and named accordingly. It is only because each of them has its specific structure in time that their growth presents that convergence of means toward an end by which we distinguish them and for which we value them. In purpose construed in this way there is evidently no need of design or intention or foresight. In making a garden there is such need. The purposes of nature may be deliberately employed to attain the purposes of men. But apart from beings

47

who foresee and plan there appears to be no evidence of intention in the world. When we speak of nature's designs, we speak figuratively, and impute to her rational and deliberate powers. But we can not clearly affirm that the rain falls in order that the garden may be watered, or that the eye was framed in order that we might see. The evidence for design of that character has been proved inadequate again and again with every careful examination of it. To say, therefore, that nature is full of purpose does not mean that nature has been framed in accordance with some preconceived plan, but rather that nature is discovered to be an historical process, the conversion of the possible into the actual in such a way that there is conserved a progressive record of that conversion.

From the selective character of history it follows that a single complete history of anything is impossible.— certainly a single complete history of the world at large. History is pluralistic. This conclusion might be reached as others have already been reached by pointing out how it follows from the purpose of writing history, and how this purpose indicates the character of movements in time. Indeed this

48

has already been done in pointing out that the history of England is its many histories and the history of a garden the history of its many seeds. Always there is a particular career and particular incidents appropriate to it. Any career may be as comprehensive as desired, but the more inclusive it is the more restricted it becomes. The history of Milton contains details which the history of English literature will omit; and the history of the cosmos shrinks to nothing when we try to write it. The only universal history is the exposition of what history itself is, the time process stripped of all its variety and specific interests. Consequently, a single purpose is not discoverable; there are many purposes. When we try to reduce them all to some show of singleness we again do no more than try to tell what a temporal order is like. It is metaphysics and not history we are writing.

To affirm that history is pluralistic is, however, only to reaffirm the selective character of history generally. A history of the world in order to be single, definite, and coherent, must exhibit a single, definite, and coherent purpose or time process. That means, of course, that it is distinguished from other purposes equally single, definite, and coherent. There are thus many histories of the world distinguished from one another by the incidence of choice or emphasis. The flower in the crannied wall with its history fully recorded and understood would, consequently, illustrate the universe. All that has ever happened might be interpreted in illumination of its career. Yet it would be absurd to maintain that either nature or Tennyson intended that the little flower should be exclusively illustrative. The wall would do as well, or its crannies, or the poet. Nature exhibits no preference either in the choice of a history or in the extent of its comprehensiveness. Man may be thought to be, and man is, an incident in the universe, and the universe may be thought to be, and the universe is, the theater of man's career.

The same principle may be illustrated from human history exclusively. We who are of European ancestry and largely Anglo-Saxon by inheritance are pleased to write history as the development of our own civilization with its institutions, customs, and laws; and we regard China and Japan, for example, as incidental and contributory to our own continuation in time. Because our heritage is Christian we date all events from the birth of Christ. Yet we gain

50

some wisdom by pausing to reflect how our procedure might impress an enlightened historian from China or Japan. Would he begin with the cradle of European civilization, pass through Greece and Rome, and then from Europe to America, remarking that in 1852 A.D. Commodore Perry opened Japan to the world? Surely he would begin otherwise, and not unlike ourselves would construe the history of the world in a manner relevant to the progress of his own civilization. Europe and America and Christianity would contribute to that development, but would not constitute its essential or distinctively significant factors. The historian is himself an historical fact indicating a selection, a distinction, and an emphasis in the course of time. His history is naturally colored by that fact. Other histories he can write only with an effort at detachment from his own career. He must forget himself if he would understand others; but he must understand himself first, if he is successfully to forget what he is. He must know what history is, recognize its pluralistic character, and try to do it justice.

To do justice to the pluralistic character of history is not, however, simply to write other histories than one's own with commendable impartiality. It is also to be keenly alive to the philosophical implications of this pluralism. The most significant of them is doubtless this: since philosophically considered history is a thing not written, but evolved and acted, to no one history can absolute superiority or preference be assigned. Absolutely considered the history of man can not claim preëminence over the history of the stars. He is no more the darling of the universe than is the remotest nebula. It is just as intelligible and just as true to say that man exists as an illustration of stellar evolution as to say that the sun exists to divide light from darkness for the good of man. Absolutely considered the cosmos is impartial to its many histories. But even that is not well said, for it implies that the cosmos might be partial if it chose. We should rather say that there is no considering of history absolutely at all. For history is just the denial of absolute considerations. It is the affirmation of relative considerations, of considerations which are relative to a selected career. There is no other kind of history possible.

The recognition of this fact does not, however, imply the futility of all history. It does not imply that any history is good enough for men since all histories are good enough for the cosmos. So to conclude is to disregard completely the implications of pluralism. If no history can claim absolute distinction, all histories are distinguished, nevertheless, from one another. If no history can claim preëminence over any other, it is true also that none can be robbed by any other of its own distinction and character. The fact that the morning stars do not sing together is not the universe's estimate of the value of poetry. The fact that the rain falls equally upon the just and the unjust is evidence neither of the impartial dispensations of deity nor of the equal issue of vice and virtue. Each event in its own history and illustrative of its own career is the law.

Yet men have been prone to write their own history as if it were something else than a human enterprise, as if it were something else than the history of humanity. Those who seek to read their destiny from the constellations ascendant at their birth are generally called superstitious; but those who seek to read it from the constitution of matter, or from the mechanism of the physical world, or from the composition of chemical substances, although no less superstitious, are too frequently called scientists. But "dust thou art and unto dust thou shalt return" is an essential truth only about the history of dust; it is only an incidental truth about the history of man. One learns nothing peculiarly characteristic of humanity from it. It affords no measure of the appreciation of poetry, of the constitution of a state, or of the passion for happiness. Human history is human history only. The hopes and fears, the aspirations, the wisdom and the folly of man are to be understood only in the light of his career. They are to be understood in terms of that into which they may and do eventuate for him, by the way in which they are incorporated into his past to make it more fully remembered and more adequately understood, and by the way they are used for his future to make his past more satisfactory to remember and more satisfying to understand.

Yet some there are who stop worshipping the stars when they discover that the stars neither ask for worship nor respond to it, and who dismiss reverence and piety when they discover that a god did not create the world. Perhaps they should not worship the stars nor believe in God, but neither astronomy nor geology affords good reasons for putting an end to human reverence and faith. If the stars have not begged man to worship them, he has begged them to be an inspiration to a steadfast purpose. It is in his history, not in theirs, that they have been divine. How stupid of him therefore, and how traitorous to his own history, if he shames his capacity for reverence, when once he has found that the stars have a different history from his own.

The inevitable failure of astronomy and geology to afford man gods suitable for his worship is not a recommendation that he should vigorously embrace the superstitions of his ancestors. To counsel that would be an infamy equal to that which has just been condemned. The counsel is rather that what is not human should not be taken as the standard and measure of what is human. Human history can not be wholly resolved into physical processes nor the enterprises of men be construed solely as the by-product of material forces. Such resolution of it appears to be unwarranted in view of the conclusions to which a consideration of what history is, leads. The obverse error has long since been sufficiently condemned. We have been warned often enough that water does not *seek* its own level or nature *abhor* a vacuum. Even literary criticism warns us against the pathetic fallacy. But in refusing to anthropomorphize matter, we ought not to be led to materialize man. We should rather be led to recognize that the reasons which condemn anthropomorphic science are precisely the reasons which commend humanistic philosophy. It is just because history is pluralistic that it is unpardonable to confound different histories with one another. So we may conclude that the pluralism of history which makes all histories, when absolutely considered, of equal rank and of indifferent importance, does not rob them, therefore, of their specific characters, nor make human history a presumptuous enterprise for them that write it not in the language of nature, but in the language of man.

This conclusion needs greater refinement of statement if it is to be freed from ambiguity. For the distinction between nature and man is an artifice. It is not a distinction which philosophy can ultimately justify. Undoubtedly man is a part or instance of nature, governed by nature's laws and intimately involved in her processes. But he is so governed and involved not as matter without imagination, but as a being whose distinction is the historical exercise of his intelligence. Nature is not what she would be without him and that is why his history can never be remembered or understood if he is forgotten. He can not be taken out of nature and nature be then called upon to explain him. As a part or instance of nature man is to be remembered and understood, but as the part or instance which he himself is, and not another. His history, consequently, can never be adequately written solely in terms of physics or chemistry, or even of biology; it must be written also in terms of aspiration.

All time processes are histories, but man only is the writer of them, so that historical comprehension becomes the significant trait of human history. To live in the light of a past remembered and understood is to live, not the life of instinct and emotion, but the life of intelligence. It is to see how means converge upon ends, and so to discover means for the attainment of ends desired. Human history becomes thus the record of human progress. From it we may learn how that progress is to be defined and so discover the purpose of man in history. For him the study of his own history is his congenial task to which all his knowledge of other histories is contributory; and for him the conscious, reflective, and intelligent living of his own history is his congenial purpose.

THE CONTINUITY OF HISTORY

ALTHOUGH history is pluralistic, it is not, therefore, discontinuous. We can not divide it in two in such a manner that its parts will be wholly unconnected. Any division we may make, although we make it as plain as the fence which divides a field, gives us a boundary which, like the fence, belongs equally to the parts on either side of it. Novelty and distinction may abound in the world, but nothing is so novel or distinct that it is wholly cut off from antecedents and consequences of some sort. It is this fact which we denote when we speak of the continuity of history. We indicate that every action of time, every conversion of the possible into the actual, is intimately woven into the order of events and finds there a definite place and definite connections. Consequently it becomes easy to represent the movement of history as a kind of progress from earlier to later things, from ancestors to descendants, or from the original or primitive to the derived. If, however, progress is to mean anything more than just this representation of historical continuity, if, for example, it is to mean, besides a progression from the earlier to the later, some improvement also, clearly a criterion is necessary, by which progress may be judged and estimated. An inquiry is thus suggested into the continuity of history to see in what sense progress may be affirmed of it and by what criteria that affirmation may be warranted. As a preliminary to this inquiry it is advisable to envisage the continuity itself and determine how far it assists in understanding what has happened.

From among the many illustrations which might be cited to bring the fact of historical continuity visibly before us, these from Professor Tylor's "Primitive Culture" are particularly suggestive because they deal with familiar things: "Progress, degradation, survival, modification, are all modes of the connection that binds together the complex network of civilization. It needs but a glance into the trivial details of our own daily life to set us thinking how far we are really its originators, and how far but the transmitters and modifiers of the results of long past ages. Looking round the rooms we live in, we may try here how far he who knows only his own time can be capable of rightly comprehending even that. Here is the honeysuckle of Assyria, there the fleur-de-lis of Anjou, a cornice with a Greek border runs round the ceiling, the style of Louis XIV and its parent the Renaissance share the looking-glass between them. Transformed, shifted, or mutilated, such elements of art still carry their history plainly stamped upon them; and if the history yet farther behind is less easy to read, we are not to say that because we can not clearly discern it there is therefore no history there. It is thus even with the fashion of the clothes men wear. The ridiculous little tails of the German postilion's coat show of themselves how they came to dwindle to such absurd rudiments; but the English clergyman's bands no longer so convey their history to the eye, and look unaccountable enough till one has seen the intermediate stages through which they came down from the more serviceable wide collars, such as Milton wears in his portrait, and which gave their name to the 'band-box' they used to be kept in. In fact, the books of costume, showing how one garment grew or shrank by gradual stages and passed into another, illustrate with much force and clearness the nature of the change and growth, revival and decay, which go on from year to year in more important matters of life. In books, again, we see each writer not for and by himself, but occupying his proper place in history; we look through each philosopher, mathematician, chemist, poet, into the background of his education, — through Leibnitz into Descartes, through Dalton into Priestly, through Milton into Homer.

"'Man,' said Wilhelm von Humboldt, 'ever connects on from what lies at hand (der Mensch knüpft immer an Vorhandenes an).' The notion of the continuity of civilization contained in this maxim is no barren philosophic principle, but is at once made practical by the consideration that they who wish to understand their own lives ought to know the stages through which their opinions and habits have become what they are. Auguste Comte scarcely overstated the necessity of this study of development, when he declared at the beginning of his 'Positive Philosophy' that 'no conception can be understood except through its history,' and his phrase will bear extension to culture at large. To expect to look modern life in the face and comprehend it by mere inspection, is a philosophy whose weakness can easily be tested. Imagine any one explaining the trivial saying, 'a little bird told me,' without knowing of the old belief in the language of birds and beasts, to which Dr. Dasent in the introduction to the Norse Tales, so reasonably traces its origin. To ingenious attempts at explaining by the light of reason things which want the light of history to show their meaning, much of the learned nonsense of the world has indeed been due." [1]

The illustrations are drawn from the domain of human interests. They could be paralleled by others drawn from natural history. The honeysuckle may carry us elsewhere than to Assyria, revealing unsuspected kinships in the world of plants. Biology has made the conception of the continuity of living forms a familiar commonplace, and geology can find in the earth's crust the story of countless years. So familiar has the idea of continuity become that terms like "evolution" and "development" have ceased to be technical and have become terms of common speech. We speak readily of the evolution of man, of government, of the steam-engine, of the automobile, and of the atom. The idea has so possessed all departments of

[1] Tylor, Edward B. "Primitive Culture." Henry Holt & Co., 1889. Vol. I, pages 17 ff.

inquiry that a large part of the literature of every subject is occupied with setting forth connections which have gone before. Not only do we go through Milton into Homer, but through yesterday into an ever receding past which grows more alluring the more it recedes. The quest for origins has been of absorbing interest. It would seem that we can never understand anything at all until we have discovered its origin in something which preceded it.

In the first lecture I pointed out how impossible it appears ever to end any history finally. We now seem to face a corresponding impossibility, namely, the impossibility of ever really beginning it successfully. It would appear that we stop only because we do not care to go farther, or lack the means to do so, and not because we can say that we have found a first beginning with no antecedents before it. We may begin the history of philosophy with the Greeks, with Thales of Miletus, but the question has been repeatedly asked, Was not Thales a Semite? Did he not derive his ideas from Egypt and Babylonia? And whence came philosophy itself? Was it not the offspring of religion which preceded it, so that, before we begin its history, we must pass, as Professor Cornford suggests,[1] from religion to philosophy? Then what of religion itself? What were its antecedents and whence was its descent? So the questions multiply interminably until we must admit that "in the beginning" is a time arbitrarily fixed or only relatively determined. History, being continuous, has neither beginning nor end.

This fact, however, ought not to bewilder any one who contemplates it steadily. It is an obvious consequence of the nature of time, for every present has a past and a future, and a first or last present is, consequently, quite unintelligible. The historian, least of all, should be bewildered. If he has recognized that history is pluralistic, he will recognize also that beginnings and ends are, in any intelligible sense, the termini of distinctions. There is not an absolute first or last in history taken as a whole, for, as we have seen, the attempt to take history as a whole, if it has any meaning at all, means the attempt to define history. It gives us the metaphysics of time, but not an absolute, complete, and finished whole, whose boundaries, although never empirically reached, are ideally conceivable.

[1] Cornford, Francis M. "From Religion to Philosophy." Longmans, Green & Co., 1912.

Our thinking moves in a direction quite different. It leads us to observe that distinctions begin and end, and begin and end as absolutely as one chooses, but do not, thereby, cut themselves off from all connections. These lectures began to be delivered last Friday, but not the day before; the first word of them was written at a perfectly definite time and place which can never be changed; they will end with a definiteness equally precise; but these beginnings and endings destroy no continuity. Every history is equally continuous, undisturbed by its beginnings and endings. Each action of time is preceded and followed by everything which precedes and follows it, and yet each action of time begins and ends with its own peculiar and individual precision. In affirming this we are affirming, by means of a particular instance, the metaphysical nature of continuity itself. For by continuity we mean the possibility of precise and definite distinctions. The continuity of a line may be divided at its middle point. It is then precisely divided, but is not, thereby, broken into two separate lines.[1] After this

[1] See Dedekind, Richard. "Continuity and Irrational Numbers," in "Essays on the Theory of numbers." Tr. by Wooster W. Beman. Open Court Publishing Co., 1901.

manner the continuity of history is to be conceived. And in the light of this conception we should understand what the continuity of history can explain.

It is tempting to say that it can explain nothing at all, but it is evident that there is an uncertainty of meaning in such a claim. For things may be explained or made clear in a variety of ways with little resemblance to one another. What we mean by a circle may be made clear by defining a circle, or by an algebraical formula, or by drawing a circle. All these ways will be fruitful, but they will be fruitful relatively to the problem which provokes them. To explain anything at all, it is necessary to keep in mind the questions to which the proposed explanation is relevant. If I am asked to draw a circle it will not do simply to define it; and if I am asked to tell what it is algebraically, it will not do simply to draw it. So it is apparent that, when we wish to know what the continuity of history can explain, or when we affirm that it explains nothing, we should have in mind, first of all, the questions to which the continuity of history would be an appropriate answer. There appears to be only one such question, and that is, What have been the antecedents of any given fact? These antecedents the continuity of history explains in that it makes them clear. It may also make clear what the consequences of a given fact have been or may be. But this explanatory value is a derivative of the preceding or an enlargement of it, through our habit of looking at consequences as derived from their antecedents, and of basing our expectations of what may happen upon our observations of what has happened. Further explanatory value in the continuity of history it seems difficult to find, even if we make the statement of it less general and more precise.

But in saying this, it is not implied that this value is mean or inconsiderable. The continuity of history is both entertaining and instructive. It is entertaining because it reveals unsuspected kinships and alluring connections. It is instructive because it furnishes a foundation for inference and practice. To man it gives the long experience of his race to enjoy and profit by. It guides his expectations and enhances the control of his own affairs. It is the same with the continuities of nature generally. They beget the vision of an ordered world and help to frame rules which are applicable in the control of nature. Accordingly it is not disparagement which is here intended, but a limitation which should be appreciated.

When we say to our children, "A little bird told me," both we and our children may be quite ignorant of Dr. Dasent's introduction to the Norse Tales. We may be quite unconscious that we are using an expression traceable to a time when people believed in such language of birds and beasts as gifted persons could understand. It may be that we repeat the words simply because we remember that our parents once successfully deceived us in our childhood by using them, and that our parents did but follow the example of theirs. But evidently we should not explain the trivial saying simply by following it back endlessly into antiquity unless we concluded that it had always been characteristic of parents to deceive children in this manner. In that case we should have discovered a metaphysical truth about the nature of parents, and no further explanation would be required.

If, however, we are not willing to admit that parents are such by nature that they will cite birds as sources of information when it is expedient to keep the real source hidden, but insist that this habit be otherwise explained, we ask for an explanation which the continuity of history alone can not afford. An explanation in contemporaneous terms is required. We do not use the phrase because our ancestors used it, although we may have derived it from them; we use it because of its known efficacy. We may, however, discover that our ancestors — or Norse parents — used it for a different reason, namely, because they believed in a language of beasts and birds. But if we ask why they so believed, it will not profit us to pursue antiquity again, unless by so doing we come upon the contemporaneous, experimental origin of that belief. For it is evident that if the belief had an origin, there was a time anterior when it did not exist, and its origin can not, therefore, be explained solely in terms of that anterior time. Its origin points, not to continuity, but to action. It indicates not that the originators of the belief had ancestors, but that, in view of their contemporaneous circumstances, they acted in a certain way. To explain the origin of anything, therefore, we can not trust to the continuity of history alone. That continuity may carry us back to the beginnings of beliefs and institutions which have persisted and been transmitted from age to age; it may reveal to us experimental factors which have shaped beliefs and institutions, but which have long since been forgotten; but it can never, of itself, reveal the experimental origin of any belief or institution whatever. That is, in principle, the limitation by which the explanatory value of historical continuity is restricted. To understand origins we must appeal to the contemporaneous experience of their own age, or to experimental science.[1]

Simple as this consideration is, it has been too much neglected by historians and philosophers in recent times on account of the profound influence of the doctrine of evolution. The great service, which that doctrine has rendered, has been to fix our attention on the evident fact of continuity from which our minds had been distracted by a too exclusive preoccupation with theories of the atomic kind. Through several centuries, philosophy had acquired the habit of thinking generally in terms of elements and their compounds, whenever it addressed itself to a consideration of nature, or of the mind, or of the relation between the two. Its principal problem

[1] If space permitted, this same limitation could be abundantly illustrated from the sciences, especially the biological sciences. They have made very clear what an essential difference there is between the continuity of living forms and the origin of new forms. This difference can be readily appreciated by comparing a work on "evolution" or "natural history" with a work on "experimental biology."

was to discover means of connection and unification which might make clear how that which is essentially discrete and discontinuous might, none the less, be combined into a unity of some sort. As it failed, it usually took refuge in the opposite idea, and attempted to conceive an original unity out of which diversity was generated by some impulsion in this initial and primal being. Philosophy thus vibrated between the contrasted poles of the same fundamental endeavor, between the attempt to combine elements into a unity, and the attempt to resolve unity into elements. The latter attempt, especially in men like Hegel and Spencer, had the advantage of involving the idea of continuity, and became the controlling philosophical enterprise of the latter part of the last century. But it was principally the doctrine of evolution or development as set forth by biologists, anthropologists, and historians that made the fact of continuity convincingly apparent and freed philosophy from the necessity of attempting to explain it. Continuity became a fact to be appreciated and understood, and ceased to be a riddle to be solved. The doctrine of evolution thus wrought a real emancipation of the mind.

But this freedom has been often abused.

Relieved of the necessity of explaining continuity, philosophers, biologists, historians, and even students of language, literature, and the arts, have been too frequently content to let the fact of continuity do all the explaining that needs to be done. To discover the historical origins and trace the descent of ideas, institutions, customs, and forms of life, have been for many the exclusive and sufficient occupation, to the neglect of experimental science and with the consequent failure to make us very much wiser in our attempts to control the intricate factors of human living. If we would appreciate our own morals and religion we are often advised to consider primitive man and his institutions. If we would evaluate marriage or property, we are often directed to study our remote ancestors. And this practical advice has sometimes taken the form of metaphysics. If we wish to know the nature of things or to appraise their worth, we are told to contemplate some primitive cosmic stuff from which everything has been derived. Thus man and all the varied panorama of the world vanish backward into nebulæ, and life disappears into the impulse to live. Not trailing clouds of glory do we come, but trailing the primitive and the obsolete.

Such considerations as these have diverse effects according to our temperaments. They quite uniformly produce, however, disillusionment and sophistication. That is the usual result of inquisitions into one's ancestry. But disillusionment and sophistication may produce either regret or rebellion. This exaltation of the past, as the ancestral home of all that we are, may make us regret our loss of illusions and our disconcerting enlightenment. It had been better for us to have lived then when illusions were cherished and vital, than to live now when they are exposed and artificial. The joy of living has been sapped, and we may cry with Matthew Arnold's Obermann

"Oh, had I lived in that great day!"

Or disillusionment and sophistication may beget rebellion. We may break with the past, scorn an inheritance so redolent of blood and lust and superstition, revel in an emancipation unguided by the discipline of centuries, strive to create a new world every day, and imagine that, at last, we have begun to make progress.

But progress is not to be construed in terms of a conservatism which is artificial and reactionary, or of a radicalism which is undisciplined and irresponsible. Conservatism and radicalism are, as already indicated, temperamental affections which a too exclusive and irrational contemplation of our ancestry may produce in us. They are born of fear or impatience, and are not the legitimate offspring of history. For historical continuity, just because it does not of itself reveal the experimental origin of any belief or institution, does not of itself disclose progress or any standard by which progress may be estimated. It teaches no lesson in morals and provides no guide to the perplexed. And the reason for this is simple. History is continuous, and, therefore, there is no point, no date, no occurrence, no incident, no origin, no belief, and no institution, which can claim preëminence simply on account of its position. If men were once superstitious because of their place in history and are now scientific for precisely the same reason, we can not therefore conclude, with any intelligent or rational certainty, that evolution has progressed from superstition to science, or that science is better than superstition. Values are otherwise determined. The continuity of history levels them all.

Yet there may be laws of history. The comparative study of history, whether the history be of civilizations or of living forms or of geological formations, reveals uniformities and sequences which promote our understanding and aid our practice. If we should find that wherever men have lived, their institutions, laws, customs, religion, and philosophy tend to show a uniformity of direction in their development, we should feel justified in concluding that the tendency indicated a law of history. Yet such laws would not be indications of progress. They would indicate rather the conditions under which progress is or can be made. For laws are expressions of the limitations under which things may be done. They show the forms and structures to which actions conform. But whether these actions are good or bad, upward or downward, progressive or retrogressive, they do not show. For decline no less than progress is in conformity with law, and the continuity of history is indifferent to both. Were we, therefore, in possession of all the laws and uniformities of history, we should not have discovered thereby what either decline or progress is; but were we in possession of a knowledge of what decline and progress are, the laws and uniformities of history would teach us better to avoid the one and attain the other.

It would seem to follow from these considerations that progress involves something more than the continuous accumulation of results in some specified direction, the piling of them up on one another in such a way that the total heap is more impressive than any of the portions added to it, and more illustrative, consequently, of a particular career. There might, indeed, be progress in this sense, if we divorced the conception of it from any standard which might intelligently judge it and set a value upon it. For the passage from seed to fruit, or any movement in time which attains an end illustrative of the steps by which it has been reached is in that sense progressive. But progress in this sense means no more than the fact of history. The career of things in time is precisely that sort of movement, and indicates the sense in which history is naturally purposeful. To call it progress adds nothing to the meaning of it unless a standard is introduced by which it can be measured. If we will risk again the treacherous distinction between man as intelligent and nature as simply forceful, we may say that progress rightfully implies some improvement of nature. We should then see that to improve nature involves the doing of something which nature, left to herself, does not do, and, consequently, that nature herself affords no indication of progress and no measure or standard of it. Nor does history afford them, if we divorce history from every moral estimate of it. For again, we may say that progress implies some improvement of history, so that to judge that there has been progress is not to discover that history by evolving has put a value upon itself. It is rather to judge that history has measured up to a standard applied to it. It seems idle, therefore, to suppose that history apart from such a standard can tell us what progress is or whether it has been made.

Yet history might do so if we are ready to admit man makes moral judgments as naturally as the sun shines. If his morality were some miracle, supernaturally imposed upon his natural career, we should need supernatural sanctions for it, for no natural achievement of his could justify it. These sanctions might justify him and what he does, if he conformed to them, but neither he nor his actions could give them natural warrant. They would express nothing after which he naturally aspires, and could, consequently, afford him no vision of a goal the attainment of which would crown his history

77

with its own natural fruition. But if his morality is natural, his ideals and standards of judgment express what he has discovered he might
be, and point out to him what his history might
attain, had he knowledge and power enough to
turn it in the direction of his own conscious
purposes. Accordingly his history then might
reveal both progress and the criterion of it.
But it would do so not simply because it is a
history, but because it is a history of a certain
kind. Man makes progress because he can
conceive what progress is, and use that conception as a standard of selection and as a goal to
be reached. He participates in his own history
consciously, and that means that he participates
in it morally, with a sense of obligation to his
career. For to be conscious implies the anticipa-
tion in imagination of results which are not yet
attained, but which might be attained if appropriate means were found. Conceiving thus what
he might be, man always has some standard
and measure of what he is. He sees ahead
of him. and moves, therefore, with care and
discrimination. All the forces and impulses of
his nature do not simply impel him on from
behind; they also draw him on from before
through his ability to conceive to what enlarge-

ment and fruition they might be carried. He condemns his life as miserable, only because he conceives a happiness which condemns it; and he calls it good, only because joys, once anticipated but now attained, have blessed it. Progress is thus characteristic of human history, because it is characteristic of man that progress should be conceived. His life is not only a life of nutrition and reproduction, or of pleasures and pains, but a life also of hopes and fears. And when hope and fear are not blind, but enlightened, his life is also a life of reason, for reason is the ability to conceive the ends which clarify the movements toward them.

"Without reason, as without memory, there might still be pleasures and pains in existence. To increase those pleasures and reduce those pains would be to introduce an improvement into the sentient world, as if a devil suddenly died in hell or in heaven a new angel were created. Since the beings, however, in which these values would reside, would, by hypothesis, know nothing of one another, and since the betterment would take place unprayed-for and unnoticed, it could hardly be called a progress; and certainly not a progress in man, since man, without the ideal continuity given by memory and reason, would have no moral being. In human progress, therefore, reason is not a casual instrument, having its sole value in its service to sense; such a betterment in sentience would not be progress unless it were a progress in reason, and the increasing pleasure revealed some object that could please; for without a picture of the situation from which a heightened vitality might flow, the improvement could be neither remembered nor measured nor desired." [1]

Carrying thus the conception and measure of progress in his own career, man can judge his history morally, and decide what progress he has made. He speaks aptly of "making" progress, recognizing in that expression that he uses the materials at his command for the ends he desires. But the materials at his command are not of his own making. He may, indeed, have modified them by former use, but in each instance of his using them they are always so much matter with a structure and character of their own. This fact puts the continuity of history in a new light. It forbids the attempt to conceive it as a movement pushing forward, as it were, into the future. We should conceive

---

[1] Santayana, George. "The Life of Reason," 1905. Vol. I, pages 3-4.

it rather from the point of view of the time process as we have already analyzed it. Then we should see that the continuity of history is the continuity of the results of the conversion of the possible into the actual — the part of the line which has been drawn. It comprises all that has been accomplished, conserved either by man's memory or by nature at large, and existing for continued modification or use. As such, it has its own structure, its own uniformities, and its own laws. To them every modification made is subject. That is why everything "connects on from what lies at hand," and why everything we do — even the expressions we use — points backward to what our ancestors have done. Since what they have done is only material for what we may do, it can not of itself explain our use of it, or judge our own values. An understanding of it should, however, make us wiser in the use of it. That is why we need contemporaneous experience and empirical science. We need to discover, either by our own experience or by reconstituting the experience of others, what happens when given material is used in a given way. Such discoveries are the only genuine explanations. They reveal the conditions to which actions must conform if the ends we desire are to be attained.

More generally expressed the continuity of history is the continuity of matter. It comprises in sum the structure to which every movement in time is subject. It makes up what we call the laws of nature conformably to which whatever is done must be done. But in itself it is inert and impotent. Activity of some sort must penetrate it, if there is to be anything effected. And what is effected reveals, when experimentally understood, the laws as limitations within which the control of any movement is possible.

A wall is built by laying stone on stone. It may be torn down and built again, or left a ruin. The placing or overthrow of every stone occurs as just that event but once, never to return, but the stones, though chiseled or worn in the handling, remain constant material for constant use. The result is a wall or a ruin, both of which illustrate the law of gravitation, but neither of which was produced by that law. That is what history is like. It is an activity which transforms the materials of the world without destroying them, and transforms them subject to laws of their own. The world is thus ever new, but never lawless. It is always fresh

and always old. The present is, as Francis
Bacon said, its real antiquity. Time is thus the
arch-conservative and the arch-radical. Forever it revises its inheritance, but it is never
quit of it.

Man's inheritance comprises both what he has
derived from his ancestors, and also the world
bequeathed to him from day to day. This
material he uses with some knowledge of its laws,
and with the conscious desire to convert it to
his own ends. The kinds of progress he can
make are thus relevant to the purposes he sets
before him. Since the satisfaction of his physical
needs and the desire of comfortable living re-
quire some mastery of physical resources, his
progress can naturally be measured by the degree
of success he makes in providing for satisfactions
of this kind. Such progress is material progress,
and its standards are economy and efficiency,
or the attainment of the maximum result with
the minimum of effort. This kind of progress is
very diversified, embracing all the economic con-
cerns of life, and much of society and the arts.
But material prosperity is provisional. To be
well-housed, well-fed, well-clothed, and even to
have friends and the opportunity for unlimited
amusement, these things have never been per-

manently regarded as defining human happiness to the full. Having these things man is still curious to know what he will do. Material progress indicates mastery of the necessities of his existence in order that he may then be free to act. If no free act follows upon such mastery, life loses its savor, and pleasures grow stale. Material progress would thus seem to be a preliminary to living well, but would not be living well itself. For man would be in a sorry plight if he succeeded in mastering the physical resources of his world, and then found nothing to do.

There seems to be nothing further for him to do than to reflect, or rather what he does further, flows from his reflections. Since he satisfies his bodily wants, not blindly, but consciously and through exercise of his intelligence, looking before and after, and trying to see his life from beginning to end, his reflections lead him to self-consciousness. He discovers his personality and makes the crucial distinction between his body and his soul. He speaks of *his* world, of *his* friends, of *his* life. He begins then to wonder for what purpose and by what right his possessive attitude is warranted; for unless he suppresses his reflections or yields himself thoughtlessly

to his instincts and emotions, he can not fail
to observe that things are no more rightfully his
than another's, and that to belong rightfully
to any one there must be some warrant drawn
from a world with which his soul could be
congenial. Even his soul begins to appear as
not rightfully his, for why should he have now
this haunting sense of belonging to another
world, and of being a visitor to this in need of
introduction and credentials? Reflection thus
gives birth to a new kind of life in which also
progress may be made. We call it rational
progress, for it involves the attempt to justify
existence by discovering sanctions which reason
can approve, and to which all should give assent,
because each soul must, on seeing them, recognize them as its own.

Reflection may lead man to do generous
things. He may comfort the distressed, help
the poor, relieve pain, or reform society. The
world affords him abundant opportunity for
his benefactions. He may create beautiful
things which he and others can enjoy perfectly
in the mere beholding of them. He may worship
the gods, dimly conscious that they at least
lead the perfect life, and that to dwell with them
is immortality. Such exercises of the spirit yield

him a new kind of happiness. But his danger lies in supposing that his existence can be thus externally justified: that others will bless him for his benefactions; that Beauty lurks hidden to be gloriously seen even at the risk of destruction; or that God intended him to be happy. If, however, he is saved from thus superstitiously converting the ideal possibilities of his life into justifying reasons why he should exist at all, he may see in them the fruition of all his history. Even his material progress gives him a hint of this, for it is genuine progress and justifies itself naturally through the attainment of its ends. For he needs no sanction to warm his body when cold, or to feed it when hungry. It is sufficient that he sees the end to be reached and finds the means to reach it. The hunger of the soul may be no less efficacious. Although these cravings tend to bring uneasiness and distaste into his animal enjoyments, they find some satisfaction if these enjoyments are idealized and transformed into a vision of what they might be freed from the material grossness which clogs them. Man then begins to conceive ideal love and friendship, and an ideal society. If only he were the free partaker of such perfect things, his existence would need no justification.

In acknowledging this, however, he may rediscover himself and learn more adequately what the purpose of his history is. It is so to use the materials of the world that they will be permanently used in the light of the ideal perfection they naturally suggest. Man can conceive no occupation more satisfying and no happiness more complete. In entering upon it he makes rational progress. Its measure is the degree of success he attains in making his animal life minister to ideals he can own without reserve and love without regret.

Human history is something more than the lives of great men, the rise and fall of states, the growth of institutions and customs, the vagaries of religion and philosophy, or the controlling influence of economic forces. It is also a rational enterprise. Expressed in naturalistic terms it is history conscious of what history is. To remember and to understand what has happened is not, therefore, simply an interesting and profitable study; it may be also an illustration of rational living. It may be an indication that man, in finally discovering what his history genuinely is, is at the same time making it minister constantly and consciously to its own enlargement and perfection. That intelligent beings should recover their history is no reason why they should repudiate it, even if they find many things of which to be ashamed; for they are examples of the recovery of the past with the prospect of a future. In reading their own history, they may smile at that which once they reverenced, and laugh at that which once they feared. They may have to unlearn many established lessons and renounce many cherished hopes. They may have to emancipate themselves continually from their past; but note that it is from their past that they would be emancipated and that it is freedom that they seek. It is not a new form of slavery. Into what greater slavery could they fall than into that implied by the squandering of their inheritance or by blaming their ancestors for preceding them? They will be ancestors themselves one day and others will ask what they have bequeathed. These others may not ask for Greece again or for Rome or for Christianity, but they will ask for the like of these, things which can live perennially in the imagination, even if as institutions they are past and dead. He is not freed from the past who has lost it or who regards himself simply as its product. In the one case he would have no experience to guide him and no memories to cherish. In the other he would have no enthusiasm. To be emancipated is to have recovered the past untrammeled in an enlightened pursuit of that enterprise of the mind which first begot it. It is not to renounce imagination, but to exercise it illumined and refreshed.

History is, then, not only the conserving, the remembering, and the understanding of what has happened: it is also the completing of what has happened. And since in man history is consciously lived, the completing of what has happened is also the attempt to carry it to what he calls perfection. He looks at a wilderness, but, even as he looks, beholds a garden. For him, consequently, the purpose of history is not a secret he vainly tries to find, but a kind of life his reason enables him to live. As he lives it well, the fragments of existence are completed and illumined in the visions they reveal.